MONEY AS PURE COMMODITY

BENJAMIN GRAHAM

MONEY AS PURE COMMODITY

MONEY AS PURE COMMODITY

Money has the aspect of "pure commodity" insofar as it consists of or is backed by one or more commodities with substantial intrinsic value. From the earliest times, money has derived either all or a good part of its value from its physical or legal relationship to monetary commodities, usually gold or silver. More recently it has appeared, conversely, that a good part of the value of both silver and gold is derived from their status as monetary metals. This latter fact suggests that a new stage in monetary technique may be appropriate, in which monetary status and pure commodity value are made reciprocally beneficial. That is, money will be benefited by commodity backing and commodities will be benefited by monetary status.

Historically, money's identification with pure commodity values falls into three stages: being first complete, then partial or fractional, and then completely absent.

The first stage is characterized by Aristotle's statement that "the substance of money should be something which is intrinsically useful and easily applicable to the purposes of life - for example, iron, silver, and the like."[1]

The emergence of gold as the primary monetary commodity, and the defeat of its rivals, seems to be associated historically with a gradual loss of emphasis on its pure commodity aspects, and its assumption of what R. H. Brand called "a certain mystic quality."[2] Thus through the ages gold appears to have transformed itself slowly from pure commodity into pure money - from the physical to the metaphysical. At a point just before

---

[1] Nicomachean Ethics, Book V.

[2] The Times (London), June 16, 1937.

World War II it threatened to lose all its contacts with human realities - at least in the Western World.

In the second stage, all forms of money are legally exchangeable for gold, but the quantity of gold available is much less than the money claims against it. Under the Federal Reserve System, prior to 1934 the relationship between our paper money and gold was about the same as that between our demand deposits and currency. In either case complete convertibility existed de jure, but de facto convertibility depended on the absence of mass conversions. In this stage the relationship between money and pure commodity has become ambiguous in several respects - including uncertainty as to how much pure commodity value resides in gold and silver.

The fractional aspect of pure commodity backing in the second stage may be illustrated by the ratio of our gold holdings to the total of currency outstanding plus "adjusted" demand deposits. (In the balance of this paper the word "money" will refer to this total.) The ratio was 18 percent in 1900, 16 percent in 1929, over 50 percent in 1940, and again at about 18 percent at the present time. I shall mention, but not dilate upon, the additional role of gold under the gold standard as regulator of both the internal credit system and the import-export flow. These functions arise, I believe, not from the quality of gold as commodity but from the formal monetary structure.

As is well known, Adam Smith and Ricardo considered a nation's stock of monetary gold and silver as akin to economic waste. They preferred a "well-regulated paper currency";[3] but they recognized that effective regulation required the obligation to redeem paper money in gold on

---

[3] Wealth of Nations, Book IV, 1. Cf. also Ricardo, Principles of Political Economy and Taxation, Ch. VIII: "A currency is in its most perfect state when it consists wholly of paper money, but of paper money of an equal value with the gold which it professes to represent."

demand. Hence in classical theory the metal reserve should be held to the minimum necessary to guarantee convertibility. But the world's inability to keep its paper money "well regulated" led inevitably to the common view that the more gold a nation held the better.

If we view the history of this second stage over a long period, we may be surprised at the success with which bank deposits and paper money have gained acceptance in place of gold and silver. Their sole advantage has been convenience; their crying disadvantage has been that they lack physical substance, and that time after time they have proved a poorer asset than their equivalent in precious metals. For long periods each of us could have held all his money in gold just for the asking, but instead we have preferred bank deposits and $10 bills. It is clear that most Americans and Britishers, at least, have had very little interest in the pure commodity aspect of gold and silver from the standpoint of joy of possession. Our interest therein has been self-protective or negative. We have desired gold only as we mistrusted paper. Whenever we could trust paper again - and often unshrewdly - we lost interest in gold.

MONEY AS PURE COMMODITY

The third stage, in which money is by choice completely divorced from commodity backing, may be said to have existed in Great Britain in the late thirties. Not only did England leave the gold standard under economic pressure - which has happened to many nations - but thereafter she definitely repudiated the principle of gold backing for her currency, as old-fashioned and inherently undesirable. Britain said clearly that she would not go back to gold even if she could - and for some years prior to World War II she could undoubtedly have returned to gold.

MONEY AS PURE COMMODITY

England has now accepted a link between her currency and gold, via Bretton Woods. There is no indication in this undertaking that the pound will be given an effective gold backing at home, or that it will have any direct tie to pure commodity values. The pound may be in fact exchangeable for gold in the open market, just as a United States government bond can be exchanged for a gold watch - but this would in no sense be a "pure commodity" aspect such as we have been discussing.

MONEY AS PURE COMMODITY

We may add that since 1933 the United States has been in some twilight zone between the second and third stage of monetary development. Legally we are now committed only to maintaining the gold equivalent for the dollar in foreign exchange - which is about the same kind of obligation as England assumes under Bretton Woods. But more explicitly, the Treasury is directed to sell gold at $35 per ounce when necessary to secure the exchange value of the dollar.

MONEY AS PURE COMMODITY

The unparalleled expansion of monetary claims during the war might well be expected to have increased the preference of Americans for physical gold as against fiduciary paper. My inquiries lead to the conclusion that there has been no appreciable hoarding of gold, although the latter was feasible in various ways. Amid all our black markets, we have never heard of a black market for gold in this country - despite its prevalence abroad. To my mind this fact is extraordinary. It indicates that within not more than a generation there has been something of a revolution in the popular attitude toward gold. The man in the street probably subscribes to the recent statement in Business Week that "actually gold derives its value from the American dollar today."[4] Not so long ago it was everyone's belief that the money of the United States derived its value chiefly from being backed by gold.[5]

The history of silver has been the opposite to that of gold. Silver has tended to lose in monetary status while it gained in industrial utility. Great Britain has just decided to abandon its thousand-year silver currency, and to melt down all its

---

[4] **Business Week, November 2, 1946, p. 10.**

[5] **See discussions of gold premiums abroad in the August 1946 letter of the National City Bank of New York. We have not space to discuss the "gold premiums" appearing in backward countries and those with depreciating currencies**

silver coins, largely in order to supply the nation's industrial needs for the metal.[6] During the last war the United States Treasury was compelled to loan out a huge amount of its monetary silver for industrial use - some 30,000 tons, of which nearly half went to the atomic bomb project.[7] By contrast, the industrial uses of gold in the war were negligible.

---

[6] Financial Times (London), September 18, 1946, p. 1.

[7] See article, "Plans to Return Borrowed Silver," Commercial and Financial Chronicle, November 14, 1946.

MONEY AS PURE COMMODITY

I should like now to refer to a possible fourth stage in the commodity aspect of money - one in which a two-way exchange is established between paper money and a composite group of basic commodities. It may be thought that this would amount to returning to a combination of the early part of stage 1 - in which many different commodities functioned as money - and stage 2, in which more money exists than monetary commodities.

MONEY AS PURE COMMODITY

In my view, however, the proposal for commodity reserve currency[8] marks a new departure in the monetary field. Its object is not so much to give commodity value to money as to give monetary value to commodities. There should be a real advantage in having our money backed in part by basic commodities -"objects applicable to the purposes of life"- for the generally bad history of unsecured and inconvertible paper money suggests that physical backing and convertibility are desirable attributes of money.

---

[8] See B. Graham, World Commodities and World Currency (New York, 1944); F. A. Hayek, "A Commodity Reserve Currency," Economic Journal, June-September, 1943; etc.

But the novel monetary aspect of the commodity reserve idea is that it is designed to benefit the producers of raw materials by giving them as a group the economic advantages now enjoyed by producers of gold and silver; namely, an unlimited market at a level price for balanced production. As a derived effect, it is designed to protect the entire economy from the baleful results of recurrent wide fluctuations in the market price of basic commodities.

The money of the future cannot again be fully identified with pure commodity values, but it can and should be related to such values. Certain key commodities should form a broad connecting bridge between the world of goods on the one hand and the world of money on the other. The flow of such key commodities into and out of monetary status can supply an important factor of equilibrium, or balance wheel, for the entire economy. As Hayek pointed out,[9] gold is no longer important enough intrinsically to perform this role adequately; and the relationship between money and

---

[9] **Hayek, loc. cit., pp. 177, 178.**

pure commodities should rest in the future on a broader base than the precious metals.

It is difficult to state categorically what advantage will accrue to the huge monetary structure of today if a relatively small amount of pure commodities are placed behind it as security. Future confidence in the dollar will depend in part on government policies recognized as sound, and in part on mass psychology. In this speaker's opinion, the placing of a quantity of basic commodities behind our money will be sound policy, and their presence will

contribute   to   a   psychology   of
confidence in our currency.

MONEY AS PURE COMMODITY

Recommended Readings

- Siddhartha by Hermann Hesse, www.bnpublishing.net

•The Anatomy of Success, Nicolas Darvas, www.bnpublishing.net

- The Dale Carnegie Course on Effective Speaking, Personality Development, and the Art of How to Win Friends & Influence People, Dale Carnegie, www.bnpublishing.net

- The Law of Success In Sixteen Lessons by Napoleon Hill (Complete, Unabridged), Napoleon Hill, www.bnpublishing.net

- It Works, R. H. Jarrett, www.bnpublishing.net

- The Art of Public Speaking (Audio CD), Dale Carnegie, wwww.bnpublishing.net

- The Success System That Never Fails (Audio CD), W. Clement Stone, www.bnpublishing.net

www.bnpublishing.net

NOTES

NOTES

NOTES

NOTES

NOTES

NOTES

NOTES

NOTES

NOTES

NOTES

NOTES

NOTES

www.ingramcontent.com/pod-product-compliance
Lightning Source LLC
Chambersburg PA
CBHW031617040426
42452CB00006B/562